MW00943590

Jean,

The Light that you already are always sees everything with crystal clarity. You are one with single-eyed vision. Remember to keep the High watch!

Blessings in Oneness,

Stephen

Condensed
Wisdom
of
Herb Fitch

— Volume Three —

Letters to
Faithful Witnesses

Stephen and Lynn Jay

ARCHWAY
PUBLISHING

Copyright © 2021 Stephen and Lynn Jay.

All rights reserved. No part of this book may be used or reproduced by any means, graphic, electronic, or mechanical, including photocopying, recording, taping or by any information storage retrieval system without the written permission of the author except in the case of brief quotations embodied in critical articles and reviews.

Archway Publishing books may be ordered through booksellers or by contacting:

Archway Publishing
1663 Liberty Drive
Bloomington, IN 47403
www.archwaypublishing.com
844-669-3957

Scripture taken from the King James Version of the Bible.

Information about the authors can be found at www.celestialnuggets.com

ISBN: 978-1-6657-0471-7 (sc)
ISBN: 978-1-6657-0472-4 (e)

Library of Congress Control Number: 2021906181

Print information available on the last page.

Archway Publishing rev. date: 04/28/2021

Table of Contents

Two Wings of an Eagle

"One wing has the capacity to receive inner direction, inner substance, inner love, inner peace. The second wing is the inner expression of God coming through manifesting as spiritual manifestation. The inner expression of the wholeness of God is revelation.

You have the power, the dominion to manifest the Word of God, and with these two wings you can fly through adversity. They lift you to transcend enmity, so you do not have to struggle against it. Through grace, those arrows and darts thrown at you are turned aside.

We find our assurance in our own spiritual experiences. We have two wings of an eagle. We have a pipeline to the inner self, and when we receive substance, we can depend on it.

We have traveled a long way in consciousness to come to the point where we can discuss these things in the quiet of oneness and know that behind the façade of humanhood stands the invisible reality, the eternal substance of God."

Herb Fitch, 1968

Herb Fitch … Beloved friend and teacher

One

Ode to Herb

"Under the guise of the Seven Letters to the Churches the path to illumination is open."

Herb's prologue 1990

"Letters to Faithful Witnesses" is a condensed version of Herb's mystical interpretation of the Revelation of St. John the Divine. We started it in November 1991 with Herb's blessing and delight as it progressed.

Our purpose was to shrink the shear bulk of the manuscript of one thousand pages of revelation tapes I had transcribed for Herb in 1988. Herb was finding resistance amongst publishers because of its length.

We set out to accomplish this without compromising the integrity or losing the fiber or quality of Herb's original, momentous work. Our original intent was to complete the twenty-five tapes of the series. However, this project was put aside when Herb launched me into the work as an Infinite Way teacher at his 1993 San Diego Easter seminar, which ushered in a tidal wave of spiritual activity.

At that time, we had completed condensing the first nine tapes into the introduction and the seven letters to the churches. It was a challenging and rewarding undertaking.

We always enjoyed going back and rereading this condensed work, and recently shared it with a few of our spiritual companions. It was so well received and welcomed so enthusiastically, that we looked again and realized it was complete and whole as is, powerfully packed to enlighten and inspire.

And so, we updated, formatted, omitted some passages, and added others. We refashioned and refined, expanding, and compacting, renaming title and chapter headings to ready it for presentation to the faithful witnesses of God.

"If I may be allowed a personal purpose it is that through this Revelation, we may feel the presence of God."

San Francisco 1968 Revelation tape

The following two letters from Herb fueled the fire we felt to condense his work. He did not accomplish the changes he wrote to me about in these letters, as his meditations, seminar schedules, and spiritual activities took his full attention. When compiling this volume, we included his instructions and followed his wishes.

* * *

DEAR STEVE:

Thank you.
I will start the tapes rolling to you toward the end
of this coming week.
I must first hear the first two or three and eliminate
long-winded introductions that belong in the prologue,
not in the body of the text. I'll take about three days
slicing off the fat so that you can work immediately with
the meat.
Christmas joy all year round to the Jays. My first
tapes are practically in your hands and I know this project
is ordained.

        ALOHA...in ONENESS,

           Herb

INSTRUCTIONS TO STEVE

✓ All of Tape #1, plus Side One of Tape #2 is being re-worked
for an introduction.

✓ John 1:1-3 of "REVELATION" is also being reworkded and will be
inserted later.

START WITH TAPE #2, SIDE #2, which is set for John 1:4 - and
which starts with the words: "John to the seven thurches which
are in Asia, Grace be unto you...." This will be Chapter One,

Once we find the rhyt-m of this, it should flow smlothly.

In November 1991 we wrote Herb:

"All we know is that we are being guided to condense the material into pure, spiritual meat; to discern it with a discriminating eye and carefully weed out the excess. Perhaps there is a need. Perhaps there are enough students who have grown in consciousness to the point where they are thirsty for pure truth; that which is undiluted and free from wordiness, thus accentuating the import and impact of the written word."

DEAR HERB:

IT IS WITH MUCH JOY, THROUGH ONENESS OF THE SPIRIT, THAT WE SEND YOU THIS COMPLETELY REWRITTEN, REVISED, EDITED COPY OF CHAPTER ONE OF THE REVELATION OF ST. JOHN.

AFTER THE NUMEROUS HOURS SPENT TRANSCRIBING YOUR TAPES, WE FEEL WE HAVE DEVELOPED A FAMILIARITY WITH YOUR UNIQUE PRESENTATION, AS WELL AS SOME DEGREE OF INSIGHT INTO THE MESSAGE OF REVELATION. WE BELIEVE YOU WILL FIND THIS CHAPTER TO BE DEEPLY INSPIRATIONAL AS WELL AS GREATLY INFORMATIVE. IT IS POWERFULLY CHARGED WITH THE DEEP REVELATION THAT FLOWED FROM YOUR CONSCIOUSNESS, GLORIOUSLY ALIVE WITH THE WISDOM SPIRIT BRINGS.

THIS CHAPTER WAS GLEANED FROM TAPES 1 AND 2 AND PUT INTO SEQUENCE WHILE RETAINING WITH FAITHFUL ADHERENCE THE ENLIGHTENING MESSAGE REVEALED. WE FEEL IT WAS CONDENSED WITHOUT COMPROMISE, WITHOUT LOSING THE FIBER OR QUALITY OF FABRIC WOVEN WITHIN THE FRAMEWORK OF THE ORIGINAL WORK. WE ALSO INCLUDED SCRIPTURAL NUMBERS AS WELL AS REFERENCES.

IF YOU BELIEVE THIS CHAPTER FEELS RIGHT WITH YOU, WHERE ONLY MINOR CHANGES MAY HAVE TO BE DONE FOR THE PUBLISHER AND WOULD LIKE US TO CONTINUE ON TO REWRITE THE REST OF THE BOOK, PLEASE ADVISE US AS WE WILL GLADLY TAKE ON THESE WORKS FOR YOU.

AGAIN, HERB, THANK YOU FOR INVITING US TO JOIN YOU AND NELL TO THE MYSTICAL ISLE OF BALI. IT WAS SO MUCH MORE THAN WE COULD HAVE EVER IMAGINED. IT WAS A DEEP SHARING FOR ALL OF US; AN EXPERIENCE IN SPIRIT AND AN ADVENTURE IN SOUL.

ALOHA FROM THE WARM AND BEAUTIFUL DESERT.

IN THE ONENESS OF SPIRIT WITH LOVE -

Dear Herb,

It's been a while, but here is Chapter Seven. I have
to say this chapter is phenominal. Every time I work on your
works I feel my body tingle. This is just dynamite, and it
will knock the socks off of any serious student. I'm not just
saying that because we're doing it. It's something that I
really feel. Anyway, Chapter Eight is in the works, and the
way things are coming along, I feel the chapters are just
getting better and better. I don't know if I can stand it
anymore. I feel electrified when I read it, and I sometimes
wonder if one day will I awaken and find myself not there
anymore? Will I look in a mirror and not see an image?

Well, San Raphal is just about around the corner.
We've also decided to stay at the Embassay Suites rather than
the Marriott so we could be closer to you and be able to
meditate and do whatever may be necessary.

See you in no time at all.

                                    With love in oneness -

8

DEAR LYNN & STEVE:

#7 felt like a rocket launch.

Steve - you were right when you said you felt the "substance" of that chapter. I did, too.

I'll see you soon.   To you and Lynn
                       and the Lamons - -
                       it will be a pleasure
                       to see you soon.
         ALOHA IN ONENESS,

This Eternal Moment

Dearest Herb,

Enclosed is the eighth chapter, "The Seventh Letter to the Churches. It is condensed, gleaned from subject matter from many of your tapes, combined with spontaneous inspiration and direction.

It feels as if this chapter ends section I of the Book of Revelation. After the Easter Seminar we will continue on with section two, incorporating into the text what is revealed by you through Spirit during this coming seminar.

We joyously await being together again in San Rafael...

                                        With Love
                                           In
                                        The Oneness
                                        Of Christ,

10

There was a mystique, a mystery around Herb in The Infinite Way discerned by those who were attuned.

In January 1996 we received a letter from an Infinite Way student who shared a pertinent and profound observation.

"It keeps coming to me that Herb will not be fully appreciated until more of the whole Infinite Way tradition comes to light. I have gotten the subtle impression that Herb, for reasons I cannot fathom, is not accepted by all of the other teachers or student body. But I am convinced that his work will really show to perfection when considered in relationship to the other unfoldments that have and are coming out."

This was our response: "As you have probably realized, Herb Fitch is a master teacher, and his circle of students are ones who spiritually discern and have a deep hunger to stretch consciousness and be fed of Soul revelation.

Your subtle impression about Herb is correct, and we have some feelings on this. First off, Herb, like Joel, did not look for human approval or acceptance. Herb looked to shake those of spiritual awareness out of their comfort zones and safety nets. He is like a bird with a song that had to be sung, and it had to be sung the way it was given to him.

Herb first met Joel at the end of 1963 and had several deep revelations during two weeks of individual study with him. It was during this time Joel asked him to go and teach and heal. In the next few months Herb received an outpouring of inner revelation, and, as such, was prepared by Spirit for his mission.

Other teachers who had been at the side of or studied collectively and individually with Joel for many years perhaps saw Herb as an intrusion, as his path was charted differently.

Herb did not stay within the confines laid down before, but broke new ground and spiraled to new heights. As Joel was a pioneer, so, too, was Herb, and his students received the fruits of that breakthrough and free flowing consciousness.

Herb took the high points of Joel's work and made that his foundation, always remaining within the perimeter of spiritual principles. He told us that, "All I taught was a branch out of Joel's teachings." He felt he poured a thimble full next to Joel's torrents. We did not feel that way, but Herb's humility is who he is.

Some of Herb's students have taken it upon themselves to transcribe his classes, and there are written works circulating. As more awaken to the depth and purity of the message revealed by Herb, we know the books will automatically follow, and those of us appointed will step forth to complete the task given with joy of purpose and fulfillment of heart."

Two

A Trio of Angels

Along our journey we have been immensely blessed to cross paths with numerous lights radiating angelic qualities. Among the many ascending beings we encountered, there was a trio of angels that greatly influenced our unfolding experience of spiritual life. They appeared to us as a selfless, angel unaware, a radiant angel of precious love, and an exuberant angel of joyous delight.

It was early in 1982 when we first met our angel unaware, Crystel Lang. Although having developed a deep, consecrated consciousness, she felt comfortable in the background, working behind the scenes as a beholder of Spirit, a true example of unassuming humility.

Crystel was a true expression of an angel unaware, a loving, selfless Soul who was tickled by Spirit. She was a faithful witness, unwavering in holding to the impersonal sense of self, while glorifying God. She did not talk about herself, and revealed nothing of her personal life, only the light she embodied.

Crystel was our introduction to The Infinite Way as an activity. She conducted serious tape groups following Joel's protocol. She was an extraordinarily, powerful Soul who humanly weighed in at perhaps eighty pounds, but with a spiritual ferocity. If she sensed an opening, she was there to nurture and feed the Soul with spiritual literature that she would photocopy for anyone that was hungry for truth.

The three of us became close spiritual friends. One day she told us she believed we were ready to meet a wonderful Infinite Way teacher of high consciousness, Muriel West Jones. She told us the day and time and could hardly contain herself, since Muriel only saw a few of the many who would have loved to study with her.

The day arrived and we met Crystel as she lovingly insisted driving us up to Muriel's home in Yucca Valley, California, where she left us and visited with some friends for a few hours. She was thrilled about our meeting Muriel, and felt she had to be there to be a part of it.

Of course, Crystel inwardly knew what meeting Muriel would do for our Soul journey and how deeply she would influence and guide us. Crystel did not speak much, but she was a knower and saw our connection from Muriel to Herb.

After Crystel passed her two sisters contacted us and told us Crystel had left us all her precious collection of books and tapes. When we picked them up, we visited with her sisters and learned a bit about the form that concealed the light that appeared as Crystel. We so admired her ability to be a clear transparency for Spirit without allowing mortal influence to enter.

One day, while talking with Herb about Crystel, we told him how instrumental she was in our life and how she held onto his very words right up to her transition in 1990. Herb pegged her perfectly when he said to us, "I know Crystel was a background person and I didn't really get to know her, but I know she was a serious student" … a description of an angel unaware.

* * *

Angelic Crystel at her confirmation, 1923

Muriel West Jones, a radiant angel of precious love, was a vision of loveliness appearing before the eyes as a mystical image of ageless, translucent beauty. She had strawberry blonde hair piled on her head and a vision of her in a pink and white gingham dress down to her ankles is etched in our minds. Looking at her you felt as though she had already transcended.

Muriel gently, but firmly prodded us along the straight and narrow path. She shared many varied experiences but was firm about not leaving the path for something, that although new and enticing, would be a diversion. She wanted us to keep our eyes on the prize and not to wavier. She taught us one who rents the veil of humanhood makes way for thousands to follow. She could not stress enough to continue climbing up the mountain without stopping all along the way. She said, "one who breaks through the mist performs a great service of love."

Mauiel taught about the Christ Circle of Brotherhood whose light assists us to become that which we already are. She urged us to keep our eye single minded, staying firm within the principles, and not to water down the message. She emphasized everything is in the process of transformation, from the smallest grain of sand to all the stars and planets in the universe.

Every month we spent hours together, talking, meditating, and listening to a tape. When we left, she would load us up with Joel's books and other mystical literature. She had a list of books which she shared she felt was necessary reading for aspiring mystics. Along with these precious books she also loaned us tapes of both Joel and Herb.

In her generosity of sharing in the Spirit she told

16

us many experiences of her incredible life. Both of her parents were spiritually aware and active in healing work and activities of the Soul. They knew her true identity as a child of God and gave her the freedom to be that. At an incredibly young age she was empowered to be all she could be and experience life without unneedful parental interference, or the aura of fearful thought or anxiety around her. She was blessed in this way and light years ahead of most of us.

We, too, were blessed to be her students. At one time she had given away all her books and tapes and had gone into seclusion to concentrate on going deeper within. Slowly she regained books and tapes and began seeing a few serious students to help fuel their ascent.

Muriel served God with an incredible, loving kindness and an exuberance rarely seen. Every pore of her being radiated love and light, and she was instrumental in our unfoldment. It was Muriel who told Herb about us, and he later shared he felt he knew us before he met us. Herb shined whenever he spoke about Muriel, about her grace and beauty, and felt anyone who knew her was blessed. Muriel was there with him from the beginning.

The words here are merely a hint and whisper to describe how deeply this incredible, beautiful Soul touched us. To us she is an ascended being with a transcendental consciousness, and more than once we found ourselves glancing at her feet to see if, in fact, they touched the ground, as she seemed to be slightly levitated above it.

Muriel was also very close friends with Betty, Herb's loving wife of more than 30 years. She told us how Betty was pure, divine love; a perfect balance to the fiery wisdom of a single-pointed genus, as we once heard Herb referred to.

Late one afternoon, after several hours of spiritual bliss, Muriel empowered us by saying that although humanly this is not what she wants, she has been inwardly instructed to let us go. She told us you are mystics in your own right. Go and be all that you can be. It was a double-edged sword as we were saddened by our treasured time together drawing to a close, and also gifted by the deep affirmation given to us that caused us to reflect and stretch.

In the year that followed she wrote and told us she was keeping close tabs on us and was delighted with all that she had heard. She wrote us, "I hear about you and rejoice in everything you see and do, as it can only be heavenward."

Muriel appeared to pass Easter Sunday, 1987 befitting a Soul of her spiritual purity.

To this day we are overcome with love by just the thought of her or mention of her name.

* * *

After San Diego, in April 1993, Herb continued his support and shared the addresses of his serious students to contact about spiritual activities. Herb also gave us the name of Alexandra Morrow to call when we arrived on Maui. He told us she was close to, studied and travelled with Joel.

Alexandra Morrow, an exuberant angel of joyous delight, was an extraordinary Soul, one that exudes childlike joy and excitement. Alexandra was simultaneously living and balancing many different lives. She was a world traveler, a spiritual seeker; studied and travelled with the mystic, Marie Watts, as well as Joel.

Alexandra excelled in Soul qualities and talent. She was accomplished at painting, sculpting, writing, teaching and was a founder of the Lahaina Arts Cultural Center.

Her home was a sanctuary for a long list of great, spiritual lights. The first time we met and meditated together she told us we were very good meditators and that we were sitting on the same couch Joel would sit on and meditate when he visited with her.

At Alexandra's home we were blessed to meet, fellowship, and meditate with Infinite Way teachers, Virginia Stephenson, Walter Starke, and Eileen Bowden with her blue, blazing eyes and strong, quiet power.

Sharing our love of God with Crystel was a grace-filled experience, as was meditating with Muriel, Herb, and Alexandra, all in exotic, spiritual retreats of intense peace and beauty. These Souls are forever gratefully emblazed in our consciousness.

Alexandra in her backyard
Lahaina, Maui

Radiance

Radiance shines when Soul
recognizes Itself as God
appearing as individualized Being.

Radiance shines when Soul
recognizes Soul as the Soul
of One and All.

Radiance - One glorious
pulsating   Soul radiating as One.

Radiance - The Glory of the Soul
awakening, Soul recognizing only
Soul and the false sense of
personality dissolving into
nothingness.

Radiance - The Heart Beat of God
is the Oness of Soul
Knowing Soul as the One and Only

Alexandra 1993

Three

Following in the
Fitch Tradition

"I am truly fortunate, for I feel as though I had been dropped into the midst of Infinite Way groups. I cannot believe the people I am meeting, and so many of them know of me, only because of Herb."

Maui, 1993

About two weeks after Herb's announcement our whole family left Palm Desert, California moving to Maui. Four generations settled in one large home. We proceeded on with our mission of Spirit, under the banner of a family boutique which has been called a front for light.

A little insight into what initially transpired when Herb dramatically altered the course of my life by the impetus he provided into the deep reservoirs of Spirit.

When Herb called me into the Infinite Way work in 1993, I was employed as an official court reporter in the Superior Court of the State of California, studying mysticism and practicing the presence. Besides meditating at intervals, I sat in long, nightly meditations between the hours of 10 pm until 2 or 3 am; slept a few hours and got ready for work. I had an hour commute, just enough time to hear a tape of Herb's. This protocol allowed me the balance and detachment needed to work in a stressful environment without disrupting my spiritual unfoldment. In addition, it was a perfect opportunity to bear witness and recognize the spiritual identity of everyone in the courtroom.

At Herb's invitation to follow in his footsteps I knew I would have to leave the security of the world for the unknown. I had the support of my family at full strength behind me. This, along with the faith placed in me by Herb, catapulted my leap of faith.

Herb knew I was leaving my job at the court and was very clear not to rely on spiritual works as a means of support. He asked me directly how I was going to make a living. When I told him our family was going to move to Hawaii and open a boutique, he simply said, "that will do it."

As a family we had no prior retail experience, but lots of accumulated faith and trust in our inner resources. We knew the gifts, talents and determination of our children, Alan, Cyndi, and Greg, and together believed we would be led.

As soon as we settled in, I began preparing for my first seminar the following year in Santa Rosa, California. After the seminars in 1994 and '95 we had the joy of visiting with Herb and are grateful to have had that quality time before he passed.

* * *

San Diego, 1995, Infinite Way seminar,
"The Purple Robe of Immortality"
Jean Mollenhauer, Seminar Coordinator and Steve

In February 1997, I received a letter from lawyers hired by the administrator of The Infinite Way, to cease and desist from teaching under the name of The Infinite Way. Although it was surprising, I complied.

I was asked to confirm in writing within 10 days which I did. The following is my letter in response to this legal action.

March 6, 1997

Robbins, Berliner & Carson
201 North Figueroa Street
Los Angeles, CA 90012
Atn: Lisa Partain

Dear Ms. Partain:

As per your letter of February 27, 1997, please note that I am not now nor have I ever been a supplier of ANY of the works authored by Joel S. Goldsmith. Furthermore, please also note that I have never used a symbol nor have I tried to mislead or represent any facts that are confusing, mistaken, or deceptive as to my affiliation or connection to The Infinite Way.

My affiliation to the way of life that is infinite speaks for itself in the light of dedication, sacrifice and the almost thirty years of walking The Path that has been traversed by all those who choose the mystic way.

In April of 1993 at an Infinite Way seminar that was given in San Diego by Herb Fitch I was introduced and called out as a practitioner and teacher by Mr. Fitch who had received his ordination in January of 1964 directly from Joel Goldsmith while together in Hawaii. I, in turn, had received my confirmation "to go and do likewise" straight from Herb. As it was, in 1994 I began giving classes based on the mystical message that was brought forth with integrity and great regard, respect and obediance to guidelines that were set down by Joel specifically for those teachers who had the consciousness to teach the message. These classes that I had given were certainly prior to any knowledge of trademarks or restrictions, as this is in direct violation and totally contrary to Joel's teachings where he writes in his description of the Infinite Way "The only restraint is the discipline of Soul, therefore we know liberty without license."

Once again, I have not now nor have I ever distributed, copied or transcribed ANY of the Infinite Way tapes or writings. I will of course continue following my unfolding destiny as a practitioner and teacher demonstrating and teaching the mystical life, but at your request will no longer do it under the banner of the Infinite Way.

Sincerely,

Stephen Jay

When reflecting on how to proceed, I took this as a sign. I was guided to retreat behind the spiritual scenes and remain on Maui, where I continued developing consciousness and being available for anyone who would call, write, or visit. I found working one on one or in small groups worked well for those who were drawn to me. It left those who were seeking better able to fill a spiritual gap, if needed.

After this unforeseen happening I quickly had a realization that this crossroad gave me a rare and precious opportunity of working together with my family as a spoke in the wheel, which I believe is a great way of refining consciousness and stimulating growth.

I remembered magnificent Muriel and her words, "it is not important what you do, but the consciousness you do it in." I also kept recalling her loving admonishment to "climb as high and straight in ways you are led because breaking through the veil can make way for thousands to follow."

It felt so right as I lived each day letting it unfold, cherishing the experience of walking together in sync with my family, which accomplished more than years of solitary study. We learned to live in, but not of the world. The fruits of this endeavor make our hearts burst in gratitude. We know of no other way that can equal the force of living and working in spiritual unison.

Many times during the day as visitors meet family members at different shop locations, we are asked about ourselves. Those who are drawn to the light often tell us we should write our family story. However, we hold our deep spiritual experiences silent, sacred, and secret, and being solitary souls for the most part, the shops are a perfect background for our family to shine the light and share a memorable experience.

I have always found whenever I have the need to talk with anyone about spiritual principles, or to sit in meditation for someone who would call, the shop would be empty allowing me the time necessary to be in the silence. Spirit works in ways we know not of when we are about the Father's business.

My works are to be a detached witness and stay out of the way; to act on Jacob Boehme's wisdom where he said, "The quickest and most direct route into the kingdom is to walk contrary to the world in all of thy ways." I take this to mean in every walk and phase of life.

Walking contrary to the world is not an easy task when one is deeply involved in business. I find it causes us at Moonbow Tropics to make decisions that would not be viewed as logical or practical, according to business sense.

Lynn and I witness the glory of a force wholeheartedly committed to living in oneness and the principles of life and have held tight and honored this way of life above all else. Love, faith, selfless cooperation, and intense, pristine energy is the bar we all hold ourselves accountable to. This is our collective purpose to manifest this time on earth.

From the vantage point of where I stand there is no delineation or separation. Spiritual work is an attitude of awareness; an altitude and atmosphere that encompasses all we are charged with doing. No two paths are the same. We all have our unique purpose, and we believe ours is to leave an account of Herb's work, as he wished, and to glorify God as a family in the life we live together.

This rare gift was one Herb recognized when, after my Santa Rosa seminar in 1994, he wrote and asked about our children and said, "you are lucky to have each other." We believe by his instructions and guidance he sparked and nurtured our spiritual testimony of grace.

It has now been twenty-eight years on Maui, and we are three generations working together. We live by combined grace and prove the truth and reality of mysticism by reaching higher and standing firmer, allowing us to impersonally move through the regulations and jump through the hoops of the world, without compromising spiritual principles.

These last decades have been revolutionary, dramatic as Soul unfoldment is. By the grace of God, we are blessed to be moved by inner promptings and impartations received directly from within. We are privileged to see hints and experience glimpses of a life lived in contemplative meditation as a continuous vibration, where the practice of the presence of God leads to the Presence living out from Soul consciousness as a living experience.

What Thou Seeth
Write in a Book

Herb's Prologue

Herb often shared with us he had been waiting on Spirit to reveal what he felt was to be the author's prologue; a concise introduction that encompassed and encapsulated what would follow as the Revelation of St John the Divine, and it eluded him.

During a trip to Bali with Herb, high in the mystical mountains of Ubad, June 23, 1990, in a deep meditation between 4 to 7 am this gushing of Spirit broke loose into form for serious spiritual aspirants to consume. This is a blessing of love from Herb to whoever reads it ...

Soul to Soul, Spirit to Spirit, Blessings of Love from the Infinite.

* * *

The life of Christ Jesus may be divided into three periods: earth life, resurrected life, and ascended life. Each period plays a progressive role in the Christ teachings. It is the third period of His life which is least known on earth.

In the interval between resurrection and ascension Christ dramatically announced that he had selected John to remain on earth after the other disciples went to higher realms. Peter, offended he had not been chosen, asked Jesus, and what shall I do? Chiding him, the Christ tells him, "If I will that he tarry till I come, what is that to thee?"[1]

Two facts are indicated: Apparently Jesus's mission was still unfinished. He had overcome the world by surviving death. Now He faced the challenge of teaching every man how to duplicate His feat. Secondly, He was focusing the eye of the world on the third period of His life.

After Christ ascended, Emperor Domitian banished John to the Isle of Patmos. On this sequestered island in the Aegean Sea, John was initiated by Christ Himself into the Rite of the Resurrection. Now, like his teacher, he had overcome the world and his Soul was prepared to perform the purpose for which he had come to earth.

Christ began communicating.

"The Revelation of Jesus Christ, which God gave unto him, to shew unto his servants things which must shortly come to pass; and he sent and signified it by his angel unto his servant John."[2]

The Eternal Voice continued to trace the path of the Illuminate, the obstacles to Sonship, the Higher Worlds, the priceless pearls of liberation into the One Life. God's perfect plan for man was revealed in fullness.

John spent many months faithfully listening and transcribing. When the last word had been spoken, John held in his hand The Gospel of the Risen Christ, a document designed to lead man from darkness to Light.

In 93 A.D. the traditional early church reviewed John's Revelation for the first time. It was not well received, and John was peremptorily branded an impostor, his work a forgery and rejected unanimously. What the council did not know was that "The Revelation of St. John the Divine" was authored from start to finish by the Risen Christ. God was the source. The Risen Christ

31

communicated it from heaven to earth. John channeled and transcribed it.

In 398 A.D., after three failures, the Council of Carthage finally accepted "The Revelation" into the Bible as Holy Canon. It took more than 300 years for The Revelation of Jesus Christ, about whom the New Testament was written, to be accepted by the Church.

In the 15th century the printing press was invented. A few bibles were circulated, but not many, and only to the wealthy people. Not until the 17th century did bibles come into the home. By then opinions had solidified. To the masses Revelation was an oddity with strange, mysterious language. To the more enlightened, the symbols and prophecies had a material meaning. The spiritual or esoteric nature of the text was only realized by a few, and not openly taught.

Today billions of mortals continue in this unawareness with many loving God with all their hearts. They obey His Commandments, they tithe, they do countless things to please Him, but they do not do what would please Him most. They do not honor the Son. This is a modern tragedy.

There is a direct relationship between infidelity to the Risen Christ and world conditions. "The natural man receiveth not the things of the Spirit of God, for they are foolishness unto him; neither can he know them, because they are spiritually discerned."3 "For who hath known the mind of the Lord, that He may instruct him? But we have the mind of Christ."4

Without the teaching of the Risen Christ the human race has the natural mind which is separated from God. Man cannot hear the Word or enter the Kingdom of God because he is a branch cut off which bears no fruit. The senses of man cannot receive the life-giving Spirit. He literally dries up and dies.

Nineteen centuries ago, Christ ascended and delivered a message to earth through John. Mankind has walked by that message and worships Jesus who performed miracles, revering Christ who resurrected overcoming death, but what about the Risen Christ? After ascension was His teaching so unimportant that man can ignore it? Who is so wise that he knows more than the eternal Christ? Who has the key to immortality? Who can teach us to make death obsolete? Who can banish sickness, hunger, and pain? Who can tame the elements? Only the Risen Christ.

The message is here for those who want it. It has been preserved verbatim through the centuries. First Christ broke the strangle-hold of world mind which keeps man mortal and earthbound. He taught that man is divine, immortal like Himself. That above the human mind there are three worlds: Soul, Spirit and Eternal Life – homogenized as one world, the world of Christ. Then, brushing past boundaries in which man has imprisoned himself, He taught divine truth to transform the world of man into the Son of God.

The Risen Christ is the missing link in man's destiny. Through His doctrine, the secret teaching He revealed, you can now find the Kingdom of Heaven.

Here is a kaleidoscopic peek at His Holy Manna contained within His Divine Revelation.

Divine Law is being violated on earth.

Divine Law will not be fulfilled until man is divine.

33

Under the guise of seven letters to the churches, the path to illumination is opened.

Counterfeit mind is the parent of material man and his problems.

Rebirth is overcoming mortality. Man translates his transient lifespan into eternity.

Advent of immortality terminates death.
Physical problems are obsolete in Divine Sonship.

Time, space, and motion are unreal

Old age impossible without time.

Man's never dying body is realized.

The law of perfection operates eternally in the never-dying body.

One Self attained.

One word in parting: "Let the dead bury their dead,"5 said Jesus. With this book we bury all dead concepts about "The Revelation." We bury prophecies about the end of the world. We bury death itself. We open our Souls to the infinite vision of the Risen Christ who invites us to enjoy the perfect universe that God created of His Own Being. At last, we walk free.

Four

A Faithful Witness

John the Beloved lived in a state of illumined awareness where all he had absorbed within culminated as a permanent dispensation. John lived in total submission to and in fulfillment of the will of God. He walked the narrow path, and, as a consequence of having pursued realization of oneness, he became the designated heir apparent, the representative of Christ Jesus on earth.

The message given now is the Word of God through Christ Jesus sent by his angel to John. And if we believe the Gospel of John, if we believe the authority of John, if we believe the words he had spoken to say that this is not my revelation but that of Jesus Christ sent to me by his angel, then we are privileged to hear what the voice of the Father, through this transparency, had to say to the world.

Christ Jesus continued guiding and instructing John, and through oneness of Soul consciousness, Jesus, through John, reveals the revelation of life, and the Book of Revelation was born.

In the language of the Soul John describes his transformation from man of earth to son of God. Cloaked in the terms of symbology, this message from the Soul is to one who can receive it. It was given to John as one who understood that this is a universe of Spirit and could look through the appearances of this world and see the Father of Light.

Our goal is to find the precise meaning of Christ's Revelation. We will to receive the Word of God from God, so we may know the meaning and find the true message of the risen Christ. We will to multiply our blessings and find the peace that we seek, and look to unearth barriers and deterrents of that peace.

A degree of clarification is received so that in all that have accepted the spiritual way of life, a firm foundation is built, so unshakable, that it prepares us to enter higher worlds than the one we know. Unless this foundation is established, we continue needlessly to suffer in duality and try to live in two worlds. It cannot be done. We will only tear ourselves apart. We cannot live in this world and in the kingdom.

The Christ message is to prepare us to step out of this world. It is exclusively concerned with making transition by accepting and believing the truth enough to live it. When we come to be God centered, we approach the possibility of transition in as much as something within us has chosen to live in such a way that transition can be obtained. We learn to prepare ourselves by an acceptance and submission to the truth as imparted.

This message of Spirit is as fresh as the day it uttered itself through John. It is a message for those who, by their way of life, are determined to serve Christ. It is for those who, through the desire to be a servant, have opened their faculties of Soul and are ready to receive, to pour, to be responsive to the inner voice. This then is the message for those who seek the ultimate glory of Christ consciousness.

*"The Revelation of Jesus Christ, which
God gave unto him, to shew unto his
servants things which must shortly
come to pass; and he sent and signified
it by his angel unto his servant John."*1

This message, transcribed by John, is a stream of consciousness. It is the Word of God through Christ Jesus. Christ is the angel of the Lord through whom John received divine communication. The indwelling presence is the angel of the Lord, a servant of the Most High, a revelator of revelation.

The word servant is very crucial. When this revelation was given to John, the word servant meant one who was committed, dedicated to pursuing the Christ message at all costs at a time of extreme persecution. This message is for those who consider themselves a servant of God. If this is your feeling about yourself, this is your message.

To be a servant of the Most High entails a complete emptying out; to be dead to the self and alive in Christ. It is to awaken, to turn and repent; to put Christ first and foremost. This is not a service in which you can divide your interests. It demands all that you are, and it gives all that it is in return.

Servants of Christ are Souls who come to a certain level of awareness which enables them to forsake all that they had believed in prior to the Christ dispensation, and to be willing to lay down their personal sense of life in their search for truth. This revelation is for that individual, whoever he or she may be, who has reached the place in consciousness where they can say, above and beyond all else, my purpose on this earth is to serve the Christ within.

37

To that individual, now as well as then, the revelation from God by Jesus, through John was meant.

*"Who bare record of the word of God,
and of the testimony of Jesus Christ,
and of all things that he saw." 2 "To
shew unto his servants things which
must shortly come to pass."3*

The things that must shortly come to pass turn out to be the why and the wherefore of all life. It helps to know that all symbols, every form of discord that appears in this revelation is not intended for a human life or to signify a physical happening. This Revelation is of the Spirit.

What we are about to see is a struggle, a mental warfare between the mind of man and the Soul. The entire activity of this revelation takes place in the mind of man fighting his own Soul. This is precisely the reason why it has not been understood. This is a struggle of ignorance of God with knowledge of God. It is a struggle of the truth and the father of lies, the hypnotism of the human mind. This is the struggle every individual goes through and has been going through in their acceptance and realization of God.

Revelation takes us on a journey dramatized by what occurs on the outer to show us what to expect to happen as we pass from one sphere to another, from one dimension to another, from one heaven to another, until we reach the seventh heaven.

*"Blessed is he that readeth, and they
that hear the words of this prophecy,
and keep those things which are written
therein; for the time is at hand."4*

You are told to hear after you read, and to keep after you hear. There is a distinction between reading, hearing, and keeping. When we read and understand the nature of what we read scripturally, that is hearing. When we understand what we read, we hear it. That is not enough, because many of us can understand, but are either unwilling or unable to find the conviction and dedication which enables us to keep what we understand. In other words, to live the Word; to live out of our understanding. There is a pyramid here, you hear or read, then understand and accept, and then live. Reading, hearing, and keeping the Word.

There comes a time, perhaps it has already come, when you can accept this way, and that will be the keeping of the word that you have heard and understood; then you are walking with God, not as an abstraction, but as the essence of life.

"John to the seven churches which are in Asia: Grace be unto you, and peace, from him which is, and which was, and which is to come; and from the seven Spirits which are before His throne."5

The seven churches are the one church of God. Each church is an out picturing of consciousness, the seven purposes of man, the seven degrees of initiation, into the realization of Christhood.

The seven churches were visible, tangible churches which had been established and were doing spiritual work. This message is veiled by addressing it to those physical churches, but it is addressing the seven purposes within.

39

Each purpose fulfilled flows into the one river of life which is the inner self, and then the outer self becomes the fruit of the inner river.

The Soul is powered by the will of God, which is called the throne of God, and before the throne, before the will are seven Spirits. As each purpose is fulfilled it opens and reveals a new gift, and these are the seven Spirits before His throne.

As we transverse the inner Christ path, one by one we attend each church within, and a purpose is fulfilled yielding another fruit, another gift, another level of spiritual awareness. The seven purposes yield seven gifts, the fruits of the Spirit called the seven Spirits.

> *"And from Jesus Christ, who is the faithful witness, and the first begotten of the dead, and the prince of the kings of the earth. Unto him that loved us, and washed us from our sins in his own blood."6*

John establishes here that because Jesus Christ was the first begotten that He is the faithful witness. We have the priceless privilege of following the one who, through being resurrected of the dead, proves to us there is a life beyond our false sense of mortality and shows us the nature of that life.

Christ Jesus is the first begotten. He is the one faithful servant who was able to rise into life eternal and to step forth back into the form to show, here, I Am, and this establishes Him as the servant of the Father, who has authority, and whose Word is the law and the power.

Before the Prince of Peace, the kings of earth are not power. There is no power in the sword, nails, or bombs. The Prince of Peace, the faithful witness, is superior to all the kings of the earth, all the powers that accompany belief in material life.

You who elect to accept the essence of God, the Christ, as your substance, are privileged to enter the kingdom behind the visible, a kingdom on earth where there is peace now, harmony now, and perfection now. There is a prince over the kings of the earth, so that all material laws of this earth are subject to that prince, and that is the Spirit of God indwelling you. Spirit will show you that it is the prince over all of those things on earth which have been a king over your human self.

You are aided in your effort to be what you are by the force that you are acknowledging. When everything that hits a consciousness that is motivated by the invisible essence is quickly seen to be a fraud, a non-existence, then you are a faithful servant nourishing your Soul with the water of the pure river of life.

The blood of Christ is the pure river of life pouring living substance from the throne or will of God. The substance is the sap of the Tree of Life flowing up and through the tree and out as the blossom and the fruit.

> *"And hath made us kings and priests*
> *unto God and his Father; to him be glory*
> *and dominion for ever and ever."7*

A priest unto God is one who receives and reflects the doctrines of God. In the inner Self, a moving river of life, the very substance of the Father flows directly into awareness, translating and blessing, and that makes one a priest of God. The Soul eclipses the human ego to reveal dominion as Spirit over this world, over land, sea and air.

> *"Behold, he cometh with clouds; and every eye shall see him, and they also which pierced him: and all kindreds of the earth shall wail because of him. Even so, Amen."*8

The Christ rising in consciousness comes with clouds, and clouds signify divine illumination, purity and perfection.

Every eye shall see Him, accept, and receive Him. Every individual on the face of the earth shall understand and will ultimately accept "I" Christ as their identity. We need no further authority for we have seen it in these words, every eye shall see Him.

Every knee shall bow, even those who have pierced Him. That includes us all, for we all have pierced the Christ of our being. We did it today and will do it tomorrow, and we keep doing it, but less and less, because we are recognizing and accepting the Christ as our inborn reality.

In this process mortal consciousness, knowing it is being pushed out, will wail. The remnant of mortal consciousness, as it becomes aware it needs to be transcended and let go, wails. When one is willing to go all the way and live as divine life, forsaking the concepts of the sense of mind, there is no more wailing for that faithful Soul.

Not by power, not by might, but by the Spirit the illusionary world tumbles down. The walls of Jericho

42

crumble. In the reality of the truth flowing from the center of your being illusion has no power. The senses are overcome. Not by force, nor by army, but by the seven trumpets; the seven inner steps of truth you follow that crumble the wall of illusion and you walk free.

Five

I Was in the Spirit

*"I am Alpha and Omega, the beginning
and the ending, saith the Lord, which
is, and which was, and which is to
come, the Almighty. I John, who also
am your brother, and companion in
tribulation, and in the kingdom and
patience of Jesus Christ, was in the isle
that is called Patmos, for the word of
God, and for the testimony of Jesus
Christ."[1]*

John, your brother and companion in tribulation, walked
on this earth in a mortal form, and had mortal problems.
He went through tribulation until he accepted that he was
not a mortal being and came into the realization of "I"
Christ as we will do.

Tribulation or Armageddon is an interior inner conflict
of doubt, a map of a struggle that happens when we are
on the threshold of eternal truth. This battlefield is a place
where even when you expect the unexpected, something
more unexpected happens.

The beauty is that the Soul cannot lose, and so we will
eventually win the battle of Armageddon. Jesus teaches
us to arm ourselves to recognize the forces of the cosmic
mind which attack our divinity with every possible disguise.

John received divine dictation on the Isle of Patmos; his consciousness made visible. The isle externalized as a place where John could be immersed in Spirit, lifted out of all sense of physicality and responsibility where he was a perfect instrument to receive and record the Word of God.

> *"I was in the Spirit on the Lord's day, and heard behind me a great voice, as of a trumpet, saying, I am Alpha and Omega, the first and the last; and, what thou seest write in a book, and send it unto the seven churches which are in Asia."2*

The Lord's day is the first resurrection of John. He tells us there came to him a transformation. That was the Lord's day for him, which is the Lord's day for each individual in their time sequence. The Lord's day for John was when he stepped out of mortality; when he completed his spiritual journey through each heaven, when in his consciousness there was a release, and he heard a voice speaking as of a trumpet.

The still, small voice is referred to as a trumpet. It is small and still, but when you hear that voice you know you hear nothing else. Still, small, and gently as it may be, at the moment It speaks that is all you hear. It blots out the entire universe. In a state of rapture, it sounded to John as clear, bright, and bold as a trumpet.

For many years John lived in a state of meekness unto the Spirit, renouncing material concepts, material tendencies, corporeality, and material ambition. John, resting in the living Word of the Father and submissive to Spirit, let the substance of God flow with the absolute confidence that substance is writing the Book of Life for him. What the substance writes becomes the Living Book of Life, and when John, through living in substance wrote the Book of Life, it was because the substance of Christ was living Its life in and as him.

Writing our book is living our life; the life we live is the book we write. What we write depends on whether we are using divine writing equipment or human, whether we are in mind or Soul, ignorance of or the knowledge of God, in the non-substance counterfeit or the substance of God. When you are conscious as "I", that which you write in your book through this consciousness is living substance, and because substance is what writes your book, your outer experience is divinity expressing.

> *"And I turned to see the voice that spake with me. And being turned, I saw seven golden candlesticks; And in the midst of the seven candlesticks one like unto the Son of man, clothed with a garment down to the foot, and girt about the paps with a golden girdle."*[3]

Everything that is said here tells us that this one appearing is the chosen one, Christ realized. All the signs say He has attained total illumination. The ankle length garment was the holiest of the holy the high priest wore in the ark. Only he who had the ankle length garment could go into the ark of the Hebrews. The chosen one is the anointed one who fulfilled the seven unchangeable

46

purposes, so he wears the ankle length garment. His garment is girdled. He is yoked to God. He and the Father are one.

> *"His head and his hairs were white like wool, as white as snow; and his eyes were as a flame of fire. His feet like unto fine brass, as if they burned in a furnace."4*

Wool is divine wisdom; the whiteness of the wool is divine wisdom and knowledge. Fire is a symbol of eternal truth. If you seek divine wisdom and eternal truth, go to him who stands in the midst of the seven candlesticks with feet like fine brass, enduring, eternal and indestructible.

> *"And his voice as the sound of many waters. And he had in his right hand seven stars; and out of his mouth went a sharp two-edged sword, and his countenance was as the sun shineth in his strength."5*

His voice is heard in the consciousness of all who are attuned in the language they understand. It is therefore referred to as many waters. The Christ speaks from the infinite, from the seven heavens to each individual consciousness in a way suited for them.

The two-edged sword is simple; accept Christ and you walk out of the deadness into life. That is one edge of the sword. Reject Christ and you remain out of heaven. That is the other edge of the sword. Acceptance or rejection by you determines which edge of the sword you experience.

You walk into heaven or you do not. You accept truth or reject it.

> *"And when I saw him, I fell at his feet*
> *as dead. And he laid his right hand*
> *upon me, saying unto me, fear not; I*
> *am the first and the last."6*

In that high moment of ecstasy when John felt and knew the Christ within himself, he fell at the feet of the Christ as dead. He is saying to us, do thou likewise. Fall dead at the feet of Christ within yourself and enter the first resurrection.

Fear not. There is only I. I am the Alpha and Omega, the first and the last. I am all there is and there has never been another. You have walked in duality and have suffered from it.

You have suffered from the belief in a self that does not exist. For always you have been the living child of the living Father created of spiritual substance, even while appearing to be walking in the false consciousness of a mortal self.

> *"I am he that liveth, and was dead;*
> *and, behold, I am alive for evermore,*
> *Amen; and have the keys of hell and of*
> *death. Write the things which thou hast*
> *seen, and the things which are, and*
> *the things which shall be hereafter; The*
> *mystery of the seven stars which thou*
> *sawest in my right hand, and the seven*
> *golden candlesticks. The seven stars*
> *are the angels of the seven churches;*

and the seven candlesticks which thou
sawest are the seven churches."7

All belief that there is such a thing as death is removed from the consciousness that knows itself to be the living life of God. This is the glorious experience which is inevitable for all the kindreds of the earth, for all eyes shall see him. You come out of the hell of belief in mortality. The key is God in you realized. The key that opens hell and lets you out, and the key that opens heaven and lets you in, is Christ realization.

The seven golden candlesticks are the seven churches. Seven stands for rebirth, transition, gold for enduring purity, and the candlesticks are the full possibilities of the gifts of God within, the unchanging purposes or capacities,

These golden candlesticks are Soul capacities, seven unchanging purposes. The seven golden candlesticks hold a candle, and that candle has a wick, and when it is aflame one finds the seven stars. The seven stars are the angels of the churches; fulfillment of the seven purposes; the seven gifts pouring forth substance.

The invisible wheel functioning through the seven gifts of God lifts you to a new level of your Soul where the seven spiritual capacities, the seven churches within, are under the government of the will of God.

The seven purposes fulfilled become one moving stream of the Father's integrated will. The living will flows as the fulness of the seven Spirits of God. The moving waters are the substance that waters the life of the faithful servants of God, bringing them into life more abundant. Then the Soul functions in the upper waters above the firmament.

Seven Letters to
the Churches

Six

Return to Thy First Love

In his revelation John addresses seven letters to the angels of the seven churches, the seven degrees of inner activity in each of us, which lead to the attainment of resurrection. John reveals these seven steps while lifting the seven veils of hypnosis.

There are seven veils clouding our perception of reality blocking the truth. One veil is unveiled at a time, and as each is removed, another gift of God flows through our Soul, until the seventh veil is unveiled, and all seven gifts unite in one river of life.

Wisdom received by the Soul unveils Christ as individual identity. The veils that separate us from that realization are the purpose of that which is revealed to us in these words of inner perception that come through John. John could receive a message that is a permanent dispensation.

The letter to the first church is happening right now, and John, through his capacity to live in the perception of Soul, is able to bring to us the first of these seven steps in this letter to the angel of the church in Ephesus.

"Unto the angel of the church of Ephesus write; these things saith he that holdeth the seven stars in his right hand, who walketh in the midst of the seven golden candlesticks."1

The first letter teaches this is a spiritual universe. Spirit is the substance of the infinite, indestructible life of God, the one life, divine existence, the invisible reality of all.

The church of Ephesus stands for divine existence; one of the gifts of the seven candlesticks, which are seven unchanging purposes. As each purpose is fulfilled, a veil is lifted, so ultimately there are seven stars, seven purposes fulfilled. The stars indicate spiritual release. And he that holds the seven stars in his right hand is he who has dominion over heaven and earth, is he who we follow, is he who we are rooted in; for he who has the seven stars knows the way to reality, the will and purpose of God.

"I know thy works, and thy labor, and thy patience, and how thou canst not bear them which are evil; and thou hast tried them which say they are apostles, and are not, and hast found them liars." 2

The false human consciousness has apostles that tirelessly serve it. It calls them sight, sound, touch, taste, and smell; the five physical senses. These false apostles are liars that present a concept according to individual perception.

Everything seen by the human mind is seen through a glass darkly and is fractured. Do not trust it, do not believe it. It is a counterfeit. The five senses interpret this world in fractions, and your life is being divided into fractions. We are now moving into wholeness. We are getting into seeing beyond this world, developing the capacity and inner persistence that is endeavoring to learn to live in eternity.

There is a tendency to come back into this world, this mixed up, tangled world which makes us feel like an outsider. We want to eliminate that tendency. The entire idea of this human experience is to walk directly through the world untouched by it and the things that come into the human mind.

In order to emerge from this world, we must pass through it, whether we want to or not. This world is our obstacle, our adversary. It is a path of thorns, and no person is exempt from this experience. We go through the earth experience, and in the process, we discover who we are, where we are, what we are to do. This is the toughening up of our spiritual resources.

"There is at Jerusalem by the sheep market a pool, which is called in the Hebrew tongue, Bethesda, having five porches. In these lay a great multitude of impotent folk, of blind, halt, withered, waiting for the moving of the water."3

Mankind lives within the five porches, the five senses, which are identical. The five senses are like porches covering the light, so the eye does not see the fullness of what is there. The five senses do not perceive the underlying reality, and in that limited sense we live bearing witness through our five senses to our own thought. In the five sense mind natural man or woman waits, blind within the five senses, lame within the five senses, having problems within the five senses, waiting for something out there to come and deliver them into, "the moving of the water."

We do not have to wait for something out there to come and free us. We have to accept Christ within, who is already an established fact, and who has overcome

53

the five senses, has overcome the world. It is Christ who delivers us out of the darkness of Egypt, and when the senses are no longer the god of this world, reigning, unchallenged and unopposed in our consciousness, we are no longer puppets of the five sense mind.

"And hast borne, and hast patience, and for my name's sake hast labored, and hast not fainted."4

Divine existence stands fast before the report of the five false apostles. Behind all that we do sustaining us, despite our moving out into a prodigal, false, human self, is the Christ. All the while we are unconsciously erring and denying our true existence, we are still the perfect, divine self, and nothing, not even our unawareness of it can change it.

"Nevertheless, I have somewhat against thee, because thou hast left thy first love."5

This is the revelation that the false consciousness has taken a wrong turn. Man of earth is out of attunement with the will of God. The entire human race is out of alignment with His will, living in a divided consciousness, a semi-conscious life in a sense mind weaving a dream of material life.

Sleeping dreams are human thought. Every sound, fear, pain are thoughts in the mind. The entire dream is made through involuntary thought. Not one single thought is voluntary.

Instead of a sleeping dream that same involuntary

54

thought works on you when you are awake, while you are walking this earth with your eyes wide open. Involuntary thought controls your life just like it did while you were in the dream.

The gamut of the human experience is a dream. As the past diminishes into nothingness, your life is filled with something vastly different than your past and the life you lived as a human being. In the realization that you are in eternity, you feel every idea in your human past was an approximate idea about your eternal being. You can go through a change of consciousness, however slow, and feel the passing nature of the experience that the façade calls your past.

As one comes to face the false beliefs of the human mind in fidelity to the Spirit within, they are a faithful witness, a true servant of God. Then it is they go forth spreading the Good News, the gospel of God. They raise the dead, those who are dead to their divinity. They heal the sick, those who are sick because they are unaware that in divinity there is no sickness. They feed the hungry, those who seek the ultimate truth and do not know that they are that truth. They do this faithfully, silently, sacredly, and secretly in their own consciousness. That is repenting, turning about, and returning to their first love by placing all trust and faith in God.

You come to discover that it is more important to seemingly fail and to trust the Father within, than to succeed without having followed inner instruction. Success without the Spirit ordaining the action is going to be false success. Failure with God ordaining the action is going to be success. It cannot fail. In other words, it may appear that you are not getting through, that you want the guidance, and it simply is not happening. If you remain in the attitude that without the guidance of God whatever you do is useless, you find your devotion to the inner self to guide you is a great asset you can develop; otherwise there is no substance, just a shallow shell of victory.

We are brought to a place where we will to live in principle, rather than respond to something outside principle. We come to not judge from the rational mind what is good to do, but rather to judge from the level of righteous judgment.

> *"Remember therefore from whence thou art fallen, and repent, and do the first works; or else I will come unto thee quickly, and will remove thy candlestick out of his place, except thou repent."6*

We repent as we turn back to our source, to our beginning, to what we originally were before coming into form. That is from whence we have fallen. We have fallen from the consciousness of I am the one, and the belief that we are not that one is the fall.

To repent is to return to the consciousness of Christ identity, our first works. It is knowing that unless I live in Christ listening, waiting, serving, and glorifying the Father, I am dead to Christ; dead to my divine existence, and the candlestick is removed.

Listen with a spiritual ear and realize that whether we willfully elect to follow the path, or through circumstance feel compelled to walk it, the inevitable outcome is the risen Christ.

"But this thou hast, that thou hatest the deeds of the Nicolaitans, which I also hate."7

The Nicolaitans is world mind, material sense, human thought, specifically in connection with the bigotry of the priesthood. It is taking the Word of God and making a formula out of it, the teaching of a doctrine that comes externally from the sense mind, not from inner inspiration. It is the teaching of those authorities on earth in the position to help lead men to Christ who do not do so, but rather erect monuments to themselves and fall into the hypnosis of their own deluded self-will. They adulterate the Christ message, divide His garment, and pierce Him because they are of a divided consciousness.

"He that hath an ear, let him hear what the Spirit saith unto the churches; To him that overcometh will I give to eat of the tree of life, which is in the midst of the paradise of God."8

The acceptance of God in consciousness opens us up to the one infinite consciousness, the perfection of being joined in everlasting oneness in the Tree of Life. That is returning to thy first love

Love flows through the Tree of Life as the sap of divinity, and the fruits of love appear on the vine of a transforming consciousness. Watch! Behold! Look and listen. Be meek unto the Father creating an inner vacuum of no thought, then divine thought flows. The living substance of the Tree of Life manifests in everyday experiences as the activity of abundance, peace and new beginnings sprouting in fertile soil.

We have a spiritual universe, not a material one. We are blessed to have an infinite, spiritual identity, not a material one, and we must maintain this in our consciousness with integrity to the Alpha and Omega ... the first and the last.

In the silence find your center and know that when you find your spiritual self it is the center of infinity. Infinity pours through that center and finds outer expression. You are not limited to your own human abilities. Nothing is impossible. The infinite Self expresses through your divine center as you live in the knowledge of the one divine life. You are given all kinds of assistance when Spirit reads your heart and sees you are committed.

In the acceptance that you are the living Spirit of God, born of the will of God, in the name, qualities, and character of Christ, the sacred alchemy of rebirth is quickened. In that knowingness the buds of your Soul open and their delicate, fragrant blossoms appear.

Into the individualized consciousness the magnitude of the qualities of Christ are realized. As one touches the chords of a piano and a sound flows forth, so do the qualities of Christ in you come into expression. It is dormant to human sense, but alive and expressing to one who knows I Am that image and likeness.

Seven

The First and the Last

*"And unto the angel of the church in Smyrna write; these things saith the first and the last, which was dead, and is alive."*1

John's second letter to the churches relays that divine individuality expresses the fruitfulness of the Spirit unto eternity. The angel of the church in Smyrna is individual Christhood within each Soul. Smyrna represents the fig industry, and figs are a symbol of fruitfulness. In the realization of divine individuality and acceptance and practice of it, one is fruitful, rich in the things of Spirit. As one sows to the Spirit within, they reap a spiritual harvest of the things begotten of God, the activity of the Spirit made manifest.

As we remain faithful to the first and the last, to the angel of the Father who holds the seven gifts, we receive the second gift, infinite, divine individuality. We live in awareness of our life as divine being, as the Spirit as our substance. The Spirit of Christ within is infinite individuality, and divine life being infinite, our individuality is infinite.

"I know thy works, and tribulation, and poverty, but thou art rich and I know the blasphemy of them which say

*they are Jews, and are not, but are the
synagogue of Satan."2*

The veil of the senses, the defects of the ego, the vanities and fears are the tribulation that causes spiritual poverty. The infinite Christ is our destiny but has not been accepted by the false human consciousness. Separated from Christ we are spiritually bankrupt. We are rich but know it not. All that the Father has contained within His being is our natural inheritance, but we do not know it.

Absence of Soul awareness in consciousness is unawareness of our source; unawareness of our Soul being one with God. And being in unawareness of our Soul, we are divided and move in a fractured consciousness, unaware we are doing it. That is the poverty mortality exists under.

Those who say they are Jews and are not is not referring to a race of Hebrews, but to a different definition of Jew. John is telling us there is no Jew, except one who strives to discover God within. One who can talk about God but who cannot demonstrate God is walking under false colors. To John, a Jew is one who is a striver for God, the Israelite, the chosen one, the elect, the one who does not follow the strict, rigid letter of the law, but follows their heart to find understanding of spiritual wisdom.

An Israelite is anyone of any religion who is a striver for God, for Christ within. It is a universal fact not separated by nations, by religions, by people. Anyone who finds the Christ is an Israelite; one who sought after and found God.

*"Fear none of those things which thou
shalt suffer; behold, the devil shall cast*

some of you into prison, that ye may be tried; and ye shall have tribulation ten days; be thou faithful unto death, and I will give thee a crown of life."3

Fear not. The ten days of tribulation are the five outer senses, which are five days and the five inner senses, which are five more days. In those ten days our five outer senses are released from their false judgments, and the five inner senses are developed. The transformation of consciousness is represented by the five outer senses and the five inner senses, the foolish and the wise.

The kingdom of heaven shall be like the ten virgins, which took their lamps, and went forth to meet the bridegroom. And five of them were wise, and five of them were foolish. And the five who were wise, the five divine senses were keeping their lamps oiled. They were in contact with the Christ within. The other five, the human senses were not. Those who live in their human senses are under the belief in mortality, while those who live through their divine senses have the knowledge of their present immortality.

In our five-sense mind looking through the finite, physical eye, hearing through the finite, physical ear, taking thought through the finite, mortal mind, we have become aware of our present level of perception instead of Soul consciousness. Remove the five senses and the single eye becomes the divine sense aware of spiritual reality. Then we are no longer in belief of mortality. We come out of the finite, into the infinite, beholding through Soul wisdom the single eye which perceives the light as the substance behind all form.

To accept the presence of infinite, divine individuality, to know that only infinite Spirit is, brings a new force to work which takes over the jurisdiction of our life. Our degree of faithfulness depends on a force, and that force is our surrender to God within.

When we are told to be faithful unto death, we are being told that we must reach the place of surrender and release where we are willing to say ... I will be totally dependent upon the activity of the Christ within. I am dying to human personality and to human dependence on material capabilities, and I place my life in the hands of Life Itself.

"He that hath an ear, let him hear what the Spirit saith unto the churches; He that overcometh shall not be hurt of the second death."4

This world and the five-sense perception are one and the same; they are the veils that appear to separate man from God. To overcome this five-sense mind is to know God aright, life eternal. If you are faithful to this unto the death of the belief in any form of separation in the one indivisible Spirit, I will give you a crown of life. The crown is an out picturing of a new sense of consciousness. It is a crown of light, of righteousness, of immortality.

A summit of purpose of the Christ message are these words: Blessed and holy is he who has taken part in the first resurrection, as the second death has no power. We are promised freedom from mortality in all of its magnitude. The prize is clear. The price for the prize will be paid only by those who recognize the validity of the prize.

62

Spirit is telling us, preparing us, building the foundation of knowledge that we may see beyond the limitation of our five senses into the many mansions that invisibly await us. In that way we are reborn into the image and likeness of God.

The recognizable signs of rebirth become more frequent. As intervals between signs become shortened, the signs become more pronounced.

Living in your Soul the divine labor pains bring great joy, incredible joy, breathless joy. You merge into all that surrounds you and it all becomes you.

The inner experience of the first resurrection is given to us to rise above material sense of life and follow the inner knower. Everything is leading us to a deeper more positive, more confident, functional realization of the life of God being born within, establishing a neutral zone that becomes pregnant with divine thought, the substance of grace.

Eight

The White Stone

"And to the angel of the church in Pergamos write; These things saith he which hath the sharp sword with two edges."[1]

This third letter fortifies faith in divine consciousness to ever maintain its spiritual life, individualizing as spiritual form. Pergamos in Soul sense means just that, the perfect qualities and divine attributes of God in Christ.

At the time Revelation was recorded, Pergamos was the seat of learning, the seat of the priesthood. It is a Greek word for citadel or fortress. We are strengthened, fortified of the Spirit to the degree we develop a citadel of faith in the Word of God.

The sharp sword has been identified previously as the two-edged sword of truth, letting one into or keeping one out of heaven. The sharp sword of Spirit has two edges, because it is necessary to cut away that which is not there to open the door to enter into a higher realm. Deep surrender dissolves unreality, breaking down concepts of matter that we may come to grow in understanding the spiritual universe. One edge of this sword keeps us out of heaven, and the other edge opens a way to spiritual progression.

"I know thy works, and where thou dwellest, even where Satan's seat is; and thou holdest fast my name, and hast not denied my faith, even in those days wherein Antipas was my faithful martyr, who was slain among you, where Satan dwelleth."2

Until the moment of transition, we continue, in some measure, to dwell in Satan's seat, where the sense mind reigns. The five-sense mind which is hypnotized by the external world is Satan's seat. This is where a sense of separation from God is conceived, originating as the false sense mind with its five false apostles. The five-sense hypnosis of this world unconsciously seeks to quench every idea and stifle every quality and tendency that can contribute to the realization of Christ within.

Material consciousness is the pinnacle of human indulgence, the center of sense gratification, and the barrier to the works of our full potential being experienced. The seat of Satan, the false human consciousness, is dead to Christ, barricaded by its own beliefs, veiling, and obscuring the truth. Whosoever dwells in a consciousness where Satan dwells believes in and witnesses a life plagued by evil and heartbreaks of all nature.

Despite the fact of our unawareness much of the time of the Spirit within, in spite of the fact we continue to tend to concentrate too heavily on the world outside, divine consciousness holds fast maintaining perfection.

Spirit remains independent of all sense impressions regardless of the appearances of the false senses. Despite how critical the appearance, no matter how lacking or limited, no matter how painful a situation or condition may seem to be, the immaculate Self is ever immaculate.

It is necessary to reach a conviction that the Spirit of God is all there is. This is essential in order to reach a new level of ourselves, only obtainable by overcoming the material consciousness of the world.

"But I have a few things against thee, because thou hast there them that hold the doctrine of Balaam, who taught Balac to cast a stumbling block before the children of Israel, to eat things sacrificed unto idols, and to commit fornication."3

Balaam was a soothsayer of a tribe called Midianites. He was called into service by Balac, the king of Moab, because the Israelites, on their exodus out of Egypt, were now coming into the territory of Moab. Balac, terrified of their numbers and power, wanted Balaam to curse them so he could defeat them.

Balac called on Balaam to curse Israel, divine truth, illumination, Christ awareness. Balac is the divided consciousness, the block for all humanity exposed. But Balaam, who waits upon the Lord for direction, is instructed to bless Israel instead. And this he does three times. Even though Balaam does not curse Israel, Balac learns how to cast a stumbling block by breaking down the purity of the Israelites; by turning them away from the wisdom of divinity, tempting them to linger in the fickleness of the five-sense mind.

What is referred to as eating things sacrificed unto idols is the food of the mind. It includes the whole complex variety of concepts congealed into a false sense of self compacted of human thought. Idols are the food of the mind, belief in the reality of matter. The natural man or woman eat of the belief that matter is reality, and quest after matter. This is mixing the purity of Spirit with the belief of matter, mixing thought, and holding belief in a five-sense physical concept of life.

At present, the image body is under the dominion of the externalization of false world consciousness. It is at the mercy of war, disease, and the forces of nature. We have little dominion over it because it is a product of a false consciousness, but as false consciousness dissolves, the infinite individualization of the divine takes dominion over the body.

The hypnotism of the human mind is the belief that the image we call body is a physical reality. And yet some two hundred years ago science revealed that the physical body is not physical at all; that the physical body is not made of flesh, but of atoms.

In our sense mind, looking at the atoms which is the substance, the fabric of cosmic thought, we make a reinterpretation into the image called matter. Flesh is the appearance the mind makes when it looks at atoms.

The physical sense of body is a reproduction of a mental image in our consciousness entertained about our unconscious concept of the spiritual body. Our consciousness forms a concept about the invisible, spiritual body, out picturing an image called physical body, an atomic, electrically charged body out picturing in time and space.

In your pre-existence, you saw with Soul vision and heard with the inner ear of Spirit. The counterfeit, the imitation, mortal mind's concept of that vision formed the appearance of a physical eye. Mortal mind's concept of hearing formed the appearance of a physical ear, and on down the body; heart, liver, lungs, all formed as an appearance to simulate an activity that was already existent in your undivided consciousness. This is the beginning of the second chapter of Genesis, the fall from divine consciousness into a self, an imitation living in a false sense of physical self, unaware of its pre-existent consciousness and its perfect spiritual manifestation of divine substance.

When we live separated from God, we live without contact with Him, without contact with the divine law, harmony, and truth of perfection. In our pre-existent consciousness all that existed was of God. Now in a second self we have imitation powers. Form without substance is valueless. You only manifest a shell, a mental form instead of a Soul form.

As you rest in the living truth, divine substance produces the visibly images, the loaves and fishes, the gold in the fish's mouth multiplied by Soul awareness.

This is conversation until from within one is given the Word made flesh, and they are in the experience of true selfhood. That is the experience of divine consciousness realized, individual consciousness and the infinite consciousness of the Father as one. Then Christ consciousness functions that life. That consciousness embraces the spiritual universe. Spiritual ideas are projected by that consciousness.

God's thoughts are the Word, the law, the perfection,

the expression of perfect ideas that express as harmony, truth and beauty, all ideas that never perish.

"Repent, or else I will come unto thee quickly, and will fight against them with the sword of my mouth. He that hath an ear, let him hear what the Spirit saith unto the churches; To him that overcometh will I give to eat of the hidden manna, and will give him a white stone, and in the stone a new name written, which no man knoweth saving he that receiveth it."4

The hidden manna, the fruit of the Tree of Life, are the secrets hidden from the five-sense mind given to those who overcome the belief in mortal sense. It is given to those who walk the earth in their spiritual body as the consciousness of the risen Christ.

The white stone is the realization of the pure, spiritual body. We receive the realization of the spiritual body, the white stone, the pure truth of Christ by perpetual, inner inspiration.

We step into the spiritual body and realize we never left. The only crossing over we have to do is to correct our thinking, the untruth that I ever was in a physical form. What happened was on the other side of the cosmic filter. This cosmic mind interpreted my spiritual body into a physical body, a physical image and put a false consciousness into it and called it life.

This must be solidified to the point that Christ portrayed to us how we are to walk through the wilderness meeting the one adversary, the carnal mind that hypnotizes us into a dream of mortality that must die.

69

Every time you go into solitude entering the womb of silence, you are being reborn into the spiritual body. In the womb of silence, the Soul inbreathes from the Spirit and feeds daily bread to the spiritual body. Your spiritual body is coming alive, and that is why you sometimes feel a new energy, a new vitality.

When you are absent from the physical form, from the physical mind, resting in the womb of silence, there is a quickening as you are fed by the inner Spirit through the Soul. Your Soul breathes Spirit just as your nostrils breath air. You feel a quickening in your spiritual body, the activity of the inner spiritual self. The more you live in the womb of silence, the more you develop the realization of your eternal, spiritual body, the garment of the Soul, the white stone.

We are in the process of converting from form to essence. Our function is to manifest the divine presence. We need to learn to move consciously in an unconditioned universe and develop our innate, spiritual capacities.

In our new consciousness we overcome hypnosis, rejecting concepts of the natural mind, bringing into play a new faculty, a discerning faculty that looks directly into the kingdom of God on earth, and we can find that discernment faculty when we refuse to trust our natural mind. It is then we experience Soul liberation from limitation in both mind and body.

We are following the Christ within that teaches us to follow life, that furnishes us with eternal life under grace. The Christ illuminates an invisible pathway. We have been given the keys to the kingdom, a kingdom of love that never fades, a peace that never ends, and bodies that do not age and do not need repair.

70

Closing out the chapter of our life in the fourth world prepares us, through Christ acceptance, to open our Soul more fully, so the Soul and Spirit merge in the unity of oneness, birthing the immaculate conception of Christ realized.

Nine

Divine River of Love

"And unto the angel of the church in Thyatira write; These things saith the Son of God, who hath his eyes like unto a flame of fire, and his feet are like fine brass."[1]

Thyatira was an ancient city of Lydia known for its purple dye. Purple is a symbol signifying inner awareness, a transcendental degree of spiritual progression, a transformation of consciousness from mind to Soul. The attainment of a consistent awareness of Soul consciousness is quickened by the light activity of love.

This fourth letter addresses the quality of love expressing through enlightened consciousness. It is a gift of the fulness of the love of the Father gradually transforming and transcending consciousness.

We find something added to our understanding of love. We learn something must be cut away. Something in us must die for the higher understanding of divine love to come into our experience, and that is the purpose of this letter to the churches.

We are mounting up the scale of love, learning to cut away the qualities which have been the barrier, freeing us from bondage to all that is contrary to perfect love.

*"I know thy works, and charity, and
service, and faith, and thy patience,
and thy works; and the last to be more
than the first."2*

Our purpose is to release infinite love into visible manifestation. We are imperfect in our understanding of the infinite love within us, but as we proceed, we expand and release concepts. The quality of love is infinite, therefore, we are in a progressive state rising from one level of releasing love to a higher level, where the last is greater than the first.

*"Notwithstanding I have a few things
against thee, because thou sufferest that
woman Jezebel, which calleth herself a
prophetess, to teach and to seduce my
servants to commit fornication, and to
eat things sacrificed unto idols."3*

Jezebel represents self-love, a quality common to all with a personal sense of selfhood. As long as there is a second self, there is self-love. The natural instinct is to preserve this self, to hold on to it, to give way of tendencies of unproductive and unbecoming behavior. The self demands and requires certain attention, moving in this world of images, expressing its will and its desire. It is an imitation of life, a pinpoint of mortal consciousness entertained by the senses and the thoughts of material mind, a barrier to divine love.

Jezebel was a Phoenician princess, married to King Ahab, the King of Israel. She stirred him up and influenced him in her ways to set up altars for the worship of her

73

god Baal. Jezebel persecuted and gave orders to kill the Lord's prophets, anyone who opposed her or believed in the one living God of Israel.

Israel, divine wisdom, man's quest for inner enlightenment was challenged by Jezebel. She was opposed by only one man, her bitter foe and adversary, Elijah, whose name means my God is I Am. He was the only one of the Lord's prophets that had not been slain, and Jezebel looked to remedy that situation. Elijah singlehandedly opposed and defeated her, revealing external prayer as meaningless, lacking divine substance.

Elijah knew that Jezebel had no knowledge of the one God, and that Christ consciousness alone accomplishes what nothing else could. He had the realization that Christ consciousness manifests as the harmony of being, as a need fulfilled, as an outer expression of the inner perfection of God. Thus, Elijah worshipped in his inner self praying for nothing in the recognition that all is already fulfilled and will appear through the spiritually toiled consciousness of a faithful servant.

In the mystical sense Jezebel, who was teaching the people of Israel to worship Baal, the symbol of external worship, is opposing Elijah, who worships in the sanctuary of the inner Spirit. This is outer worship and inner worship, material consciousness and spiritual consciousness, the many idols without and the one living God within, brought face to face.

Elijah had ascended the seven degrees of consciousness and completed the seven steps of initiation and lived in the seventh heaven of eternal wisdom. The truth he knew within is the truth he proved without. Elijah had developed the ability to stand still and behold the salvation of the one divine life expressing through enlightened being.

Elijah lived in obedience and inner attunement to the still, small voice, and no outside influence could move him. It had been revealed to him that God is not in the external forces, no matter how powerful or fearful they may appear. He lived in the one divine life, and that one is the one God he worshipped. This inner recognition is the law of immunity experienced by Elijah and those of like mind.

> *"And I gave her space to repent of her fornication; and she repented not. Behold, I will cast her into a bed, and them that commit adultery with her into great tribulation, except they repent of their deeds."*4

This is a call to action, a new set of rules, a change of priorities. There is a break with yesterday, so that all bondage to pass habits of world consciousness that are clinging, trying to override the higher impulses, are carefully weeded out and transcended by inner purification.

One life is the only life established long before we appeared in form. That life is the life that the world calls Jesus. That life is the life that the world calls you, and our growing awareness as that life and the qualities of that life lift us out of self-love to unfettered, unbiased, love divine.

> *"And I will kill her children with death; and all the churches shall know that I am he which searcheth the reins and hearts; and I will give unto every one of you according to your works."*5

75

Everything that is conceived out of our human accomplishment is a child of self-love. All the children of self-love, the children of personal selfhood, are condemned to death as they are created of mind substance, which is temporal and dying.

The children of divine love, the children of Soul sense, are prospered. The deeds of that self are ordained. The Spirit goes before the children with its power functioning in the invisible purpose fulfilled by eternal, spiritual substance.

The individual degree of truth lived in one's life determines their experience. Each manifest according to their attained measure of Christ realization, the degree they are radiating in Christ love or in bondage to self-love; in Spirit or personal me.

"But unto you I say, and unto the rest in Thyatira, as many as have not this doctrine, and which have not known the depths of Satan, as they speak; I will put upon you none other burden."6

There is a place one comes to where the tide turns, where no other burden will be put upon them because they are putting forth the dedicated spiritual effort necessary to live in remembrance of spiritual selfhood. This assures one of being under the government of God, under the grace of God, free from bondage to the law of karma.

"But that which ye have already hold fast till I come. And he that overcometh, and keepeth my works unto the end, to him will I give power over the nations."7

He that overcomes will receive power over the nations, over all material beliefs of the world. The descent of the Holy Spirit quickens one from the consciousness of dying creature to the consciousness of the light of Christ.

This is a way we know if we are being faithful to the works of the Father, faithful to the activity of Christ within. By now we should be alerted that we are not keeping His works whenever we find ourselves swimming in the undertow current of separate selves, bearing false witness, perpetuating the dream.

It is then we do whatever it takes to rectify this by getting back into the realization that the only life there is is the life of God. This is accomplished by deep love and enlightened faith which transcends the obstacle of separate mind images.

"And he shall rule them with a rod of iron; as the vessels of a potter shall they be broken to shivers; even as I received of my Father."8

All powers in this world are shattered as the vessels of a potter thrown upon the ground by the truth which is the rod of transmutation. The truth of Spirit maintained in consciousness dissolves false appearances of power.

"And I will give him the morning star. He that hath an ear, let him hear what the Spirit saith unto the churches."9

The morning star, the day star, is the illuminating light of Christ coming through as a beacon, a lamp bestowing Soul vision. The morning star is the rising, the birth of

Christ in consciousness as one awakens from the mortal dream. In the stillness of the Soul and confidence in the Spirit the morning star rises in consciousness, illuminating, enlightening, and blessing.

The spiritual self is the center of an infinite universe. All of infinity pours into and through the divine river of love into expression through the center of one who lives in the knowledge of that which is divine.

The scales are changing; where mortality weighed the most heavily first it has now been over balanced by the conscious awareness of immortality.

Ten

Be Watchful

"And unto the angel of the church in Sardis write; These things saith he that hath the seven Spirits of God, and the seven stars; I know thy works, that thou hast a name that thou livest, and art dead."1

This fifth letter concerns all of us. This is where we measure ourselves against the truth. We can take inventory and see where we are. We see where we are succeeding and where we are falling short and what we are going to do about it.

You may find at this point in your pilgrimage you are wondering just how far you really can go. You wonder do I have the capacity? Even though I am told that God is infinite, and God individualizes as every being, as the one being made visible, do I really have the capacity to do what I will to do?

You may feel perhaps I retained enough. I reached a level where I am quite satisfied. There can be many things going on in your mind, and this is the time to look in the mirror and face the facts of being.

Take a letter, says the Spirit to John. This dictation comes from Christ Jesus. It is from He who governs the seven heavens. We are being told we are a seven-fold being, and the seven stars are our unfulfilled faculties, latent within us in the seat of Christ.

It now comes to us to accept that He who holds the seven stars, He who governs the seven Spirits and has attained the full realization of sonship with God is speaking to John, saying, take a letter to the angel of Christ within every being.

The fifth letter speaks of the secret of omnipotence. God is the only power in His eternal creation. The fifth gift granted is spiritual dominion over the entire material universe.

The Sardis is a precious stone representing omnipotence, the all power dominion over this world. In Exodus we learn that Moses was told to construct the breastplate of the high priest in a way that the Sardis stone was the first stone on the first row, depicting a high spiritual designation.

A high priest is one who has fulfilled the four unchanging purposes and has stepped into the fifth level, that of Soul consciousness. It is one who is able not to be pressured by the thought of this world, and to remain immune and unmoved by it.

As one rises in Soul awareness, they no longer believe in the reality of human beings created of flesh and blood. These evaporate as they exist as images in mind consciousness. By the grace of Soul consciousness, one may behold the grandeur of spiritual forms comprised of indescribable, resplendent hues of radiant light.

> *"Be watchful, and strengthen the things which remain, that are ready to die; for I have not found thy works perfect before God."2*

It is necessary to clarify that no matter how high or far one seems to have risen in consciousness they are not to be overly satisfied. They are not to feel honorable, but honored to be a vehicle, not the source or possessor, but the instrument through which Spirit expresses.

Be watchful is the command. We are strengthened by the wisdom to know that world thought, the cosmic mind is functioning and weaving its web of hypnosis. We can stop duality and division by relying on Soul discernment. In the realization of God as the only power, in love of the presence of God as the only presence, mountains of illusions dissolve. Soul vision can nothingize whatever problem the human sense portrays.

To watch is to be awake, to strengthen the things that remain that we have become conscious of. It is to throw off every shackle of concept, not to be pre-committed, not to be foresworn, but rather to be free to be chosen by the Father.

We learn that one of the pre-requisites to freedom is the willingness to be committed to Christ in the midst of all. That is the commitment the Spirit acknowledges; the commitment to Christ that ushers in the freedom for the unexpected divine impulse that leads to an unseen, unsuspected realm of consciousness, where the prefect works are experienced.

The precious stone of Sardis is attained as we let the human mind drift by like a cloud and rest in the pure, infinity of being, seeking nothing, asking for nothing, knocking on nothing.

"Remember therefore how thou hast received and heard, and hold fast, and repent. If therefore thou shalt not

watch, I will come on thee as a thief,
and thou shalt not know what hour I
will come upon thee."3

World thought sneaks in like a thief entering when our guard is down, when we are not fortified in Spirit, not consciously alert. Repent or perish. Yield and overcome. Turn back to spiritual awareness, to spiritual identity, to a spiritual universe, and know conscious oneness with source. The remembrance of living in awareness of the perfection of being is holding fast.

It does not matter if at this moment the voice is not booming within you, or the Tree of Life is not blooming within. Hold fast and repent. Turn back to spiritual awareness, to identity, to a spiritual universe.

In Sardis we are being liberated from world mind, united into the realization of the one perfect divine and only mind, maintaining its perfect universe.

"Thou hast a few names even in
Sardis which have not defiled their
garments; and they shall walk with me
in white; for they are worthy. He that
overcometh, the same shall be clothed
in white raiment; and I will not blot out
his name out of the book of life, but I
will confess his name before my Father,
and before his angels. He that hath an
ear, let him hear what the Spirit saith
unto the churches."4

There is a place when you cut all ties walking out on the waters of Spirit and prove you are a priest of God. You wear the Sardis stone in the front row of your breastplate, and you say, Father, thy will be done. I am dead to self-will, to personal desire, to seeking and striving and struggling. I am dead to sense desire. I am dead to all that which is not the Christ, and in the deadness to that which is not Christ am I alive in Christ.

To the degree one consciously walks in truth, living out of the new emphasis, to that degree have they transferred authority from sense mind to Soul consciousness. To that degree have they kept their garments spotless. When one accepts their name, their spiritual identity as I am, as the fullness of Spirit where they stand, they are clothed in white raiment, the divine substance of the spiritual body, and receive the white stone.

The inbreathing of the Soul of spiritual substance establishes the finished garment of the Soul body as one's permanent self; the body that walks through this human experience immaculate, untouched, expressing the activity of spiritual consciousness.

Eleven

Divine Substance of Wisdom

"And to the angel of the church in Philadelphia write; These things saith he that is holy, he that is true, he that hath the key of David, he that openeth, and no man shutteth; and shutteth, and no man openeth."1

The sixth letter to the church in Philadelphia, Christ, through John, addresses the quality of divine wisdom, divine thought, omniscience, the sixth gift of the Spirit to those who live in the will of God.

The sixth letter imparts that divine wisdom manifests through a Soul that is rooted in the will of God. The wisdom of divine inspiration projects its perfection into consciousness making itself known in response to dedication to the will of God.

Divine wisdom is revealed by the words of faithful witnesses endowed with an awareness of truth: of Soul perception ordained by Spirit to speak the glad tidings. When we are attuned, we may hear divine impartations direct. The words of Christ filter through the Soul when the mind is free of the conflict of self-will, free of worldly wisdom.

In ascending degrees of conscious oneness with God, divine wisdom is received translating as principles revealing the will of God that you can cleave to, learn from, and grow by. As you practice the principles you feel your spiritual muscles growing and discover new levels of awareness are opening within the realm of your Soul.

You can look at things that hitherto had been forbidding, discouraging, and maybe despairing, and you can find some assurance within yourself that what you once accepted as real now somehow shows itself to be an image in thought. As you live by principles revealed, the wisdom of the Father flows as grace externalized by substance.

When through transcendental consciousness you become aware of the Spirit present where you are, and the Soul pours forth its light, no man can bind it. It is loosed by your Soul, and no power on earth can oppose it successfully. The work accomplished by enlightened consciousness is the bridge, the instrument through which divine wisdom flows, going before you and preparing the way.

> *"I know thy works; behold, I have set before thee an open door, and no man can shut it, for thou hast a little strength, and hast kept my word, and hast not denied my name."*2

There is an open door for you to walk through into Soul consciousness, into heaven on earth. You walk through the open portal by fulfilling the function of providing an open vessel to receive and carry forth the will of God. There is a completely new sense of awareness. You become non-reactive, non-resistant; more aware of a force moving through your being, invisibly following the will of God.

> *"Behold, I will make them of the synagogue of Satan, which say they are Jews, and are not, but do lie; behold, I will make them to come and worship before thy feet, and to know that I have loved thee."3*

Some of the numerous residents of the synagogue of Satan include self-love, self-will and self-absorption, all offspring of mortal belief. What challenges us is our inability to weave through the intricate lies, deceptions, and assumptions that have formed a somewhat impenetrable veil to those of us who seek within.

We find growing confidence even though we stumble. At least we are moving in the direction of Spirit, which is far better than feeling successful in the material world, and then later find all you had gathered is a mirage.

> *"Because thou hast kept the word of my patience, I also will keep thee from the hour of temptation, which shall come upon all the world, to try them that dwell upon the earth. Behold, I come quickly; hold that fast which thou hast, that no man take thy crown."4*

When one steps out of self will into the willingness to do God's will, "I" come quickly with the sword of truth, with the power of truth, with the magnificence of spiritual fruitage. The crown of righteousness is achieved by holding fast, by remaining true to Soul sense above the evidence of material sense. By standing in truth revealed, one finds their defense against the world.

Think back a moment when truth first came to you in a strong way and you got onto your white horse. You had a bow and were given a crown and went forth to conquer. You had the truth; you had the crown of victory, you had the bow and you had a target, and you could not miss. You were exalted beyond the power of your imagination. You felt as though you were dashing off into a new horizon, because you had the truth, the awareness of a certain power within, and you set out to conquer. And this is what happens when truth first enters in and lifts you out of the prison of a human mind. What a glorious feeling it is.

Then, lo and behold, you find another horse emerging and you do not consciously want to, but you change horses. You come off of the white horse onto a red one, and then onto a black one, and then onto a pale one.

You began on a white horse of truth, ready to hit a perfect bullseye. You have a crown of victory. What happened? On the red horse there is another rider, war. On the black horse there is another rider, famine. On the pale horse there is another rider, death. The false world consciousness tricks you into reacting emotionally, intellectually, and physically.

The war, famine, and death symbolize what is taking place within us. Each of us has a war going on and rides the red horse of turmoil and inner unrest; taking place because of the nature of human emotions.

The black horse is the famine of the intellect, the sense of reason and logic, the five-sense mind. It is black because it is not of the light.

The pale horse is belief in matter, the consciousness of body, of form, of death.

And so you find that although you have accepted and believe the Word and started out on a white horse, a power unknown to you moves through you. It is the world mind which takes you off the white horse of truth into a bed of emotions; emotions you would rather not have. This is the red horse you do not want to ride but are provoked. Things happen, and despite the truth you leave the white horse of purity and are in a state of reaction. There is nothing you can do about it at the moment, until it comes to your awareness it has happened.

The red horse, the carnal mind, moves us out of the truth we thought we were riding, and now we are riding on emotions. We are riding on the belief that there is something out there that deserves our indignation, anger, or resentment; something that we do not like and need to condemn.

Along comes a wave of world thought and we are not on a red horse anymore. Now we are in the famine, the cold logic of our reason and intellect. We are on the black horse, and it is the polar opposite of the white one. Whereas we started out riding the white horse, the light of truth, now we are reasoning our way. We are in the five-sense mind, material consciousness, fooled by the appearance called matter. Our intellect is what we are riding on now that with our mind we can figure it all out. That is the famine.

The fourth horse, the pale horse, is even harder to overcome, for it is acceptance of the physical world. You start out on the white horse with the desire to follow the message of Christ Jesus, but the world mind comes to

88

you and you encounter beliefs which appear as horses; the red horse of emotion, the black horse of intellect, the pale horse of matter; all denials of the fact that God is all.

Eventually the white horse is going to overcome the other three. But first you go through acts of purification. You overcome the red horse, the war of emotions. You overcome the black horse, the famine of the intellect. You overcome the pale horse, death; all belief in mortal life.

> *"Him that overcometh will I make a pillar in the temple of my God, and he shall go no more out; and I will write upon him the name of my God, and the name of the city of my God, which is new Jerusalem, which cometh down out of heaven from my God; and I will write upon him my new name. He that hath an ear, let him hear what the Spirit saith unto the churches."*5

Enlightened consciousness worships the Father. Through the wisdom of Christ awareness, one is a pillar in the temple of God, and they go out no more. This is their last incarnation. There is no need to go out of the spiritual universe into physical form when Christ rises in you. The Soul receives and showers forth the light of Spirit, and you now walk in your luminous body of Soul; the perfect wedding garment. You are now equipped to live in the eternal, in the City of New Jerusalem, the City of My God, the city of Light.

The light within consciousness externalizes forming itself as a divine image walking under grace. Things that are needed appear, for the intelligence of the light becomes the law. Living from the invisible center you are the light itself, and that light appears outwardly showing forth the harmonies of divine thought, the wisdom of God as it moves through your consciousness.

There is another world out there, a universe, a different light than the light of the sun. The inhabitants of that world travel in light bodies, fed by the infinite, under divine jurisdiction of God government.

Twelve

Gold Tried in the Fire

Mystically speaking in the esoteric language of the Soul, the first letter unveils mortal creation teaching this is a spiritual universe. Spirit is the substance of the infinite life of God, the one invisible reality of all.

The second letter unveils the poverty of mortal self, revealing that fruitfulness is experienced as divine individuality is expressed. Infinite life is the divine individuality of Spirit expressing infinity unto eternity.

The third letter unveils the illusion of mortal selfhood, mortal qualities and form, fortifying faith in divine consciousness, ever maintaining its spiritual life, embodying divine attributes, the perfect qualities of God.

The fourth letter unveils the diversion of self-love addressing divine love, the activity behind transformation; the fullness of the infinite love of God.

The fifth letter unveils the illusion of mortal power revealing the secret of omnipotence; dominion over the universe is the nature of spiritual power.

The sixth letter imparts the illusion of world thought by revealing divine wisdom manifests through a Soul that is rooted in the will of God. The wisdom of divine inspiration expresses in response to dedication to the omnipotence of God.

*"And unto the angel of the church of
the Laodiceans write; These things
saith the Amen, the faithful and true
witness, the beginning of the creation
of God."1*

The seventh letter unveils the illusion of separate dying
selves. It speaks to the quality of divine righteousness,
conceived out of living in true identity, in fidelity to God
realization. In Laodicea, a city of conventions, all forces
are gathered in realization of I Am.

Amen indicates fruition. Here in the seventh letter, the
six having gone before, we have the Amen, or He who has
travelled these seven steps writing this letter to you, and
he is the faithful and true.

*"I know thy works, that thou art
neither cold nor hot; I would thou wert
cold or hot. So then because thou art
lukewarm, and neither cold nor hot, I
will spue thee out of my mouth."2*

Lukewarm is that state where we are neither cold
nor hot. It is that in-between state in which we are
undecided. We are not fully dedicated and pause along
the way, willing to go at our own pace, and do our own
business instead of the Father's pace, and the Father's
business.

We cannot serve two masters, because if our
consciousness is divided it will fall. Matter and Spirit do
not mix, for Spirit functions only in a spiritual form through
the vessel of the Soul.

There is a tendency to settle, to be satisfied with

92

crumbs. We either tread water or launch out into the deep. We tread water by not making our commitment. We launch out into the deep by making and honoring our commitment.

Truth reveals we have a function, a great, wonderful, glorious opportunity to release our divinity into daily expression; to be clear channels for the will, power, grace, and love of God. We have assistance in this bold venture into truth, the Living Word of God. We need divine truth, for it is only truth that can roll back the stone of ignorance and let in the light of life that unites us with God. Divine truth opens the door of the cave and releases the captive.

Soul replaces mind perception, mind manipulation, and behold, without effort, with patience and knowledge of inner truth, we receive a quick readjustment. There comes the quickening of understanding in a moment of realization where an exquisite feeling of living substance is flowing. In that moment you have the divine impulse, and in that moment, infinity is functioning as you in consciousness.

"I counsel thee to buy of me gold tried in the fire, that thou mayest be rich; and white raiment, that thou mayest be clothed, and that the shame of thy nakedness do not appear; and anoint thine eyes with eye salve, that thou mayest see. As many as I love, I rebuke and chasten; be zealous therefore, and repent."3

When we learn to live by inner revelation by the Word of God guided by His will, this is gold tried in the fire.

As we resolve to walk in Christ, we become sensitive

to a lot of other things. This will feel like chastisement, and will appear as renewed trials, amplification of problems. Disguised as an intensification of problems it is really a drawing closer to Soul discernment.

Your Soul is what your mind is to your body. The mind receives impulses and guides the body. The Soul receives impulses of God which are transmitted by Christ to Spirit through Soul. Soul is the channel through which the body of Spirit functions. Soul is the connection between Christ and this world. In Christ, your Soul functions as your mind does in your physical body, only on a vast infinite scale.

Your substance is the Spirit of God; your mind is the consciousness of God; your body is Spirit, permanent awareness. It is living without personal sense, without responding to the evidence of the senses, and of upholding the truth of your being which continues the purification process of trying gold in the fire.

Your Spirit always has a table prepared for you if you are standing in your identity. Through the magic pipeline of Christ all that you need is provided. Substance translates into all added things building strength and dependence in your own spiritual identity for all things, so you become self-existent. Your needs are met through the resources of spiritual identity, and the confidence of this built on is the experience of this.

The Word of God comes through your Soul as His living expression. All the beautiful things that come through grace are powered by the Soul itself and substantiated by the Spirit. These are enduring. These are real. These carry with them the stamp of divine power.

*"Behold, I stand at the door, and knock:
If any man hear my voice, and open
the door, I will come in to him, and
will sup with him, and he with me. To
him that overcometh will I grant to sit
with me in my throne, even as I also
overcame, and am set down with my
Father in his throne."4*

We have hearkened to His voice, opened the door, and now sup with Him. Let us stretch our spiritual wings and fly beyond this world, beyond the known into the unknown, living beings without boundary. Let us cleave to spiritual identity, imbued with Soul substance seated on the throne of the will of God expressing grace in all ways.

Those of us who walk arm in arm are a very special household with a purpose to move through the multitudes as disciples of divinity, first attaining and then sharing our attainment quietly and silently.

Whosoever overcomes and lifts the seven veils comes to dwell as one who has an ear, meek unto the will of the Father, taking inner dictation from the Spirit, bringing out deeper capacities and greater potentialities of Soul expression.

*"He that hath an ear, let him hear what
the Spirit saith unto the churches."5*

There is a communication method whereby the living Spirit dwells upon the keyboard of the seven churches within playing a new kind of melody. It unites the churches into incredibly, wonderful combinations interwoven in the silence established within.

There is a broad beam of silence like a vast bar of music filling all time and space. All notes become as one note, and it seems to move, it seems to quietly ring, drawing the entire universe into a vast chord of silence.

List of Scriptural References

Herb's Prologue

1 John 21.22
2 Rev 1.1
3 1 Cor 2.14

4 1 Cor 2.16
5 Matt 8.22

Chapter Four

1 Rev 1.1
2 Rev 1.2
3 Rev 1.1
4 Rev 1.3

5 Rev 1.4
6 Rev 1.5
7 Rev 1.6
8 Rev 1.7

Chapter Five

1 Rev 1.8-9
2 Rev 1.10-11
3 Rev 1.12-13
4 Rev 1.14-15

5 Rev 1.15-16
6 Rev 1.17
7 Rev 1.18-20

Chapter Six

1 Rev 2.1
2 Rev 2.2
3 John 5.2-3
4 Rev 2.3

5 Rev 2.4
6 Rev 2.5
7 Rev 2.6
8 Rev 2.7

Chapter Seven

Chapter Eight

Chapter Nine

Chapter Ten

Chapter Eleven

Chapter Twelve